CLOTHES & CRAFTS IN

ROMAN TIMES

Philip Steele

A ZOË BOOK

A ZOË BOOK

© 1997 Zoë Books Limited

Devised and produced by
Zoë Books Limited
15 Worthy Lane
Winchester
Hampshire SO23 7AB
England

First published in Great Britain in 1997 by
Zoë Books Limited
15 Worthy Lane
Winchester
Hampshire SO23 7AB

A record of the CIP data is available from the British Library.

ISBN 1 86173 000 4

Printed in Belgium by Proost N.V.
Editor: Kath Davies
Design & Production: Sterling Associates
Illustrations: Virginia Gray

Photographic acknowledgments

The publishers wish to acknowledge, with thanks, the following photographic sources:

Lesley & Roy Adkins Picture Library 19b; Ancient Art & Architecture Collection 10t; Corinium Museum, Cirencester 7t; C.M.Dixon 3, 4, 5, 6, 7b, 8, 9, 10b, 12, 13, 14, 15t, 16, 17t & br, 20, 21, 22, 23, 24, 25; Mansell Collection 18; Werner Forman Archive 17bl / Metropolitan Museum of Art, New York title page, 11 / Museo Nazionale Romano, Rome 15b / Museo Barracco, Rome 19t.

Cover: C.M.Dixon - all photographs.

The publishers have made every effort to trace the copyright holders, but if they have inadvertently overlooked any, they will be pleased to make the necessary arrangement at the first opportunity.

CONTENTS

INTRODUCTION

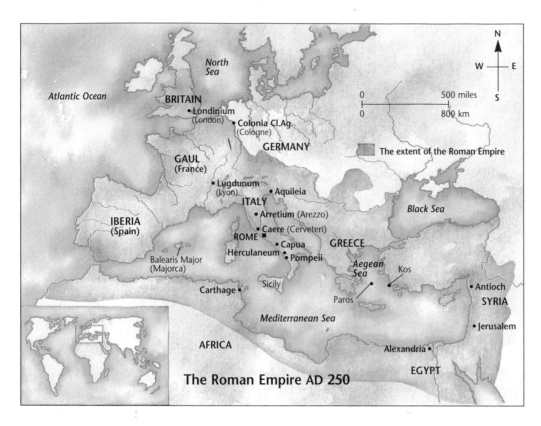

The Roman Empire AD 250

◀ The lands of the empire provided the Romans with gold and silver, iron, timber and stone. All these are called raw materials, because people make other things with them. The Romans could buy in, or import, ivory from Africa, woollen cloth from Britain and silk from the Greek island of Kos. They could sell, or export, Roman goods right across their empire.

Many different peoples were living in Italy about 2500 years ago. Greek people settled in the south and on the island of Sicily. They brought skills with them from their homeland. They were fine potters, weavers and metalworkers. They made their cities beautiful with statues and with a gleaming, polished stone called marble.

The Etruscan people lived to the north, between the Rivers Arno and Tiber. They were famous for their brilliant gold and silver work, their wall paintings and pottery.

At this time, Rome was only a small hillside settlement in western Italy. But as the years passed, the Romans became more and more powerful. By 290 BC they

▼ This Etruscan woman and man are made of a baked clay called **terracotta**. They were modelled about 2500 years ago. The model was found in a tomb at Cerveteri. The Romans copied many of the craft skills of the Etruscans.

◀ This picture of Roman women is more than 1900 years old. It shows clothing, jewellery, furniture, wall decoration and pottery.

By studying ancient crafts, we can discover how people lived long ago. We can find out how objects were made, who made them, and how they were sold and used.

controlled all of central Italy. By AD 100 they ruled a vast **empire**. It stretched from Britain to Syria, and from North Africa to the shores of the Black Sea. The Roman empire lasted until AD 476.

People who are skilled at making things with their hands are called **craft** workers. The Romans learned many of their craft skills from the Greeks and from the Etruscans. They also picked up new ideas from other peoples they conquered, such as the Celts of northern Europe and the Egyptians.

There were few machines in Roman times. Useful everyday items were made by hand. Roman craftworkers also produced beautiful works of art, including glass, jewellery and pottery. We still admire this work today.

Craftworkers in Ancient Rome

The city of Rome was noisy with hammering and sawing from workshops. Craftworkers were called *fabri* in the Latin language. Most of them were men. Each craft had its own organization, or guild.

● There were jewellers, ivory carvers, pearl setters and ring sellers.
● There were workers of gold, silver, copper, bronze and iron.
● There were carpenters and woodcarvers, and workers in marble or stone, called stonemasons.
● There were fur workers, called furriers, leatherworkers, boot and shoe makers.
● There were weavers, tailors, cloak makers, embroiderers and dyers.

ROMAN CRAFTS

Pottery

Today, our bowls, plates, cups and jugs are mostly made of pottery or china. The Romans also used pottery plates, dishes and other tableware. Rich people dined off bronze or silver plates.

Roman vases and the big storage jars that people used for oil or wine were all made of pottery. So were small, oil-filled lamps, toys and small statues. Many homes had pottery wall decorations, called **reliefs**.

People who study the things which other people made or built long ago are called **archaeologists**. They have found Roman pottery which shows us how ordinary people worked, played, cooked food and lit their homes in Roman times.

Roman potters made very large storage jars from slabs of clay. They pressed the clay around a wooden frame. Smaller pots

▲ German drinking beakers were often glossy black. Some of them were decorated with a white liquid clay, called slip.

◄ This style of red pottery is sometimes called Samian ware. It became popular after about AD 100.

were shaped, or 'thrown', on a potter's wheel. As the wheel spun round, the potter's fingers and thumbs shaped the wet clay. Some pots were shaped in a clay **mould**, which gave them a decorative pattern. When the pot had dried out, it was placed in a hot **kiln** and baked hard.

◄ This model shows what a pottery workshop would have looked like in Roman times. One worker is bringing fresh clay to the potters. They are shaping new pots on their wheels. The pots are left to dry while another worker puts firewood into the kiln.

▲ This is a reconstruction of a Roman kitchen showing a variety of pottery that the Romans used for storing and serving food.

Many different sorts of clay were used to make pottery. The colour and the quality of the clay depended on the local supply. The finest pottery in Italy was made around Arretium (modern Arezzo) from about 100 BC. Later, Roman Gaul (France) became the biggest centre of pottery production.

Dining in style

● Plain **earthenware** was very cheap. Many local potteries made it.

● Arretium pottery was expensive. It was coral-red with a glossy shine. This pottery was often decorated with pictures.

● Potters in Roman Gaul used a hard clay which was also red, but slightly darker than Arretium pottery. It was exported all over the empire.

● The areas around the Rivers Rhine and Moselle, in Roman Germany, produced jugs and beakers for export. They were decorated with mottoes such as *BIBE* ('Drink!'), *REPLE* ('Fill Up!') and *DA VINUM* ('Bring Wine!').

The remains of potters' workshops have been found all over the Roman empire. Some workshops were like small factories. They employed dozens of workers, who turned out hundreds of thousands of pots in a year. Many pots were stamped with the maker's **trademark**.

▼ Potters were sure of a job in the Roman empire. The Romans who settled in distant lands needed local supplies of plates, storage jars and oil lamps.

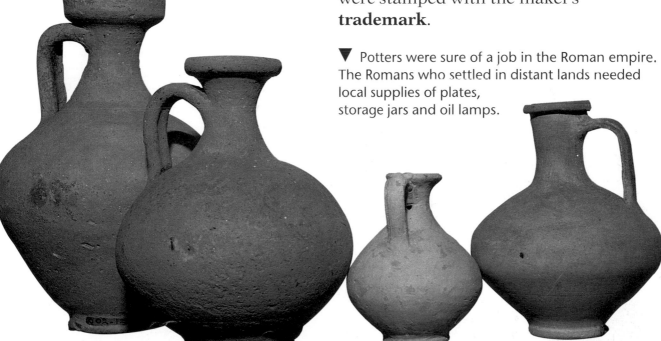

Glassmaking

The Romans used glass to make drinking glasses, bowls, drinking bottles and perfume flasks, as well as brooches and all kinds of jewellery. Cheap glass trinkets were for sale on the streets, but many luxury items must have cost a fortune. Glass tableware became more common in the later years of the empire.

The Romans made glass from sand, **soda**, and **lime**. These raw materials came from Cumae in southwest Italy, from Gaul, Spain (Iberia) and the Near East. The glassmakers mixed and then melted these materials in **furnaces**. The hot liquid, or molten, glass was poured into moulds or coated around a central shape, and then cooled.

Letting in the light

● Windows and room screens were made up of small pieces, or panes, of glass. In most houses the windows were covered by animal skins or by wooden shutters. Only the richest Romans could afford to use glass for their windows.
● Thick glass skylights were used for some public buildings, such as the baths in Pompeii and Herculaneum.

▼ The Romans made delicate, beautiful glass. Some of it can still be seen in museums. Some pieces were very simple. Others were cut into lines, or ribs, or twisted into spirals. The glass was usually blue-green in colour. Sometimes **minerals** were added to make it silvery or coloured. Other glass was **gilded** or painted with designs. These Roman glass flasks were found in Nîmes, France.

▲ A Roman drinking cup, or goblet

From Rome to Venice

● The town of Aquileia was the centre of glassmaking in Italy. In AD 452, when the Roman empire was coming to an end, fierce invaders called Huns destroyed the town.
● The people of Aquileia fled to the islands and lagoons of the coast. There they later built a new town, called Venice.
● The people passed their craft skills on to their children. Venice became the centre of European glassmaking for hundreds of years.

Sometime after 100 BC the Syrians, from the eastern part of the Roman empire, learned a better way of shaping molten glass. They blew it into shapes using a long tube. Syrian cities and the Egyptian city of Alexandria were famous for their glassmakers.

Cologne, on the empire's German frontier, also became a centre for glass-making. Many pieces of Roman glass have the trademark CCA stamped on them. It stands for *Colonia Claudia Agrippinensis*, the Roman name for the town.

▲ The jug above was made by blowing glass.

▶ The tall jug was made from strips of glass. It was not blown like the jug on the left of it.

Woodwork

The lands of the Roman empire included vast forests. Today these woodlands have mostly disappeared. They provided all kinds of hard and soft timbers, from the oaks of northern Europe to the famous cedars of the eastern Mediterranean.

Every town and village in the Roman empire had its woodworkers. Carpenters sawed wood for the building trade and for the army and the navy. Joiners made furniture for the home. Woodcarvers decorated furniture and screens with elaborate patterns and designs.

Wood, unlike pottery, glass and stone, will rot away over time. However, we do know what Roman woodwork looked like. There are pictures of it in many ancient paintings and stone carvings.

We can also learn about Roman woodwork from recent **excavations** at the Roman towns of Pompeii and Herculaneum. When the nearby volcano Vesuvius erupted in AD 79, ash and boiling mud covered the

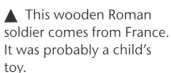

▲ This wooden Roman soldier comes from France. It was probably a child's toy.

◄ A boat builder uses an **adze** to shape the timbers of a Roman ship. A modern woodworker would recognise a Roman woodworker's tools. They included **chisels**, hammers, **planes**, saws, axes, rulers and **drills**.

towns. Everything which burned away left a shape in the cooling ash. Archaeologists found that if they filled these hollow shapes with plaster or plastic resin, they could make a copy of the original objects.

Excavations show that most Roman houses had less furniture than our own. The tables were often small and round, and many had three carved legs. Paintings do show Roman women sitting on beechwood armchairs, but benches and carved stools were much more common. Woodcarvers often decorated cupboards, chests and door panels. Many window screens and shutters were made of criss-cross, or lattice, work.

▲ This bed is a masterpiece of the woodcarver's art. It is decorated with figures and inlaid with ivory and precious stones. It comes from Pompeii.

Fancy woods, fancy prices

● One of the Romans who died when Vesuvius erupted in AD 79 was Gaius Plinius Secundus, or 'Pliny the Elder'.

● Pliny was interested in plants, including trees. He wrote about trees, timber and the uses of different woods.

● Pliny tells us how Roman joiners imported fashionable woods from North Africa. Their customers paid huge sums of money for these woods.

▲ A blacksmith hammers out a sheet of iron on his **anvil**.

Metalwork

The Romans needed large amounts of raw materials to run their empire. This was one reason why they invaded so many other countries. The British Isles had valuable mineral **ores**, such as tin, lead, copper and gold. Gaul could provide copper, lead, zinc and iron. Spain also had rich **deposits** of tin, gold, silver, lead and copper. Germany offered plentiful supplies of iron ore.

▼ This ingot, or pig, of lead was produced in Britain. It has the mine owner's name stamped into it. Lead went through several smelting processes. There was silver in this ore, which was taken out by smelting.

Slave labour

● Prisoners and slaves had to work in the mines under terrible conditions. Many of them died in rockfalls and floods. The ore they mined was carried to the surface in baskets.

● Gold dust was washed from crushed ore and melted down. Iron and lead ore was **smelted** in furnaces. The metals were made up into bars called ingots. Some metals are mixtures, or **alloys**, of other metals. Bronze contains copper and tin, brass is made of copper and zinc, and pewter is a mixture of tin and lead.

Many everyday items were metal. There was a **blacksmith** in almost every town and village and in every **legion** of soldiers. He hammered out tools, weapons and pots and pans, and he re-used, or recycled, any scrap metal.

▶ A Roman bronze statue of Vulcan

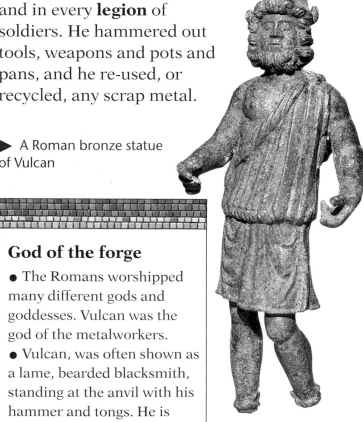

God of the forge

● The Romans worshipped many different gods and goddesses. Vulcan was the god of the metalworkers.

● Vulcan, was often shown as a lame, bearded blacksmith, standing at the anvil with his hammer and tongs. He is similar to the Greek god Hephaistos.

▲ These cutlers are selling all kinds of tools and knives. Roman metalworkers made everything from kitchen knives to locks.

Smiths were often highly skilled craftsmen. They produced beautiful ornaments and dishes of gold, silver and copper. Metalworkers made fine bronze furniture, lanterns and **cutlery**. The workers who made reliefs and statues out of metal were especially skilled. They turned metalworking from a craft into an art.

Some cities, such as Capua in Italy and Lugdunum (now Lyon) in Gaul, were famous for silver and bronze work of the highest quality.

▶ The Roman empire needed metalworkers for everything from kitchenware to silver coins. Even the simplest saucepans, such as this bronze cooking pot, were often beautifully made.

▲ This helmet and face mask was made of bronze. It would have been used for games and displays of skill by army officers on horseback. **Armourers** and weapon makers were skilled workers in both iron and bronze.

Stonework

Many Roman buildings such as bridges, public baths and temples still stand today. The Roman architects and engineers who designed and built them were very skilled.

Among the craftworkers who made these buildings so beautiful were the stonemasons. The best stonemasons had an artistic feeling for the stone they worked with. The columns holding up the roofs of many public buildings were skilfully carved. The walls were decorated with bands, or **friezes**, of gods and goddesses or historical events. Marble statues were placed in public places and in private gardens.

Pick and polish

● Many different types of stone were quarried in the Roman empire. Marble was the best stone for carving. It came from the Greek island of Paros, from the Spanish island of Majorca and from Carrara, in Italy. Carrara still produces Europe's finest marble.

● Quarry workers split the stone away from the rock face with picks, wedges and crowbars. They cut it into blocks using iron saws and shaping tools called adzes.

● Ox-wagons or boats carried the blocks to the stonemason's yard. Here, stonemasons used hammers and chisels to shape and carve the stone. Finally, they polished the stone with sand.

▼ This stone carving is part of Trajan's Column. It shows Roman soldiers building a fort on the northeastern frontier of the empire, beyond the River Danube.

One famous carved marble column, more than 30 metres tall, stood in the centre of Rome. The Emperor Trajan (AD 53-117) ordered it to be made. Trajan's Column is decorated with scenes from army life. They have given historians all kinds of fascinating clues about how people lived in ancient Rome. We can see details of clothing, shoes, haircuts, weapons and armour.

The mason's masterpiece

Trajan's Column is made of 17 huge pieces of marble. They were quarried on the island of Paros. There are 23 curved stone panels, which together show 2500 human figures!

▲ This carving was found at Carthage, a Roman city in Tunisia. It is the top, or capital, of a stone pillar. Stone has survived better than most Roman craft materials. However, later builders often stole stones from old Roman buildings to re-use.

◄ A Roman stonemason carved this scene on a stone coffin, or sarcophagus. It shows the musicians in a funeral procession. Only a very rich person could afford such a fine coffin.

Mosaics

The Romans decorated their walls, floors and ceilings with pictures. Some of these pictures were made from small chips of coloured glass, stone or pottery. They are called mosaics.

The mosaics in the houses of rich Romans often showed hunting scenes or bowls of fruit. One house owner in Pompeii had a mosaic floor at his front door. It showed a fierce dog and the warning in Latin, *CAVE CANEM* ('Beware of the dog!'). Temples and public buildings had the finest mosaics. They showed patterned designs or pictures of the gods.

Sometimes mosaics were put together in a workshop. Then the finished picture was cemented in place. Most mosaics were made where they would be on show. The base of the picture was a layer of rubble. It was levelled and covered in cement. Then a wet lime paste was spread on. The thousands of tiny chips, called *tesserae*, were carefully pressed into this plaster, which hardened as it dried.

▼ This fine mosaic shows a charioteer holding a horse. He wears the racing colours of his sponsor. Mosaics like this one would have been made for wealthy sports fans.

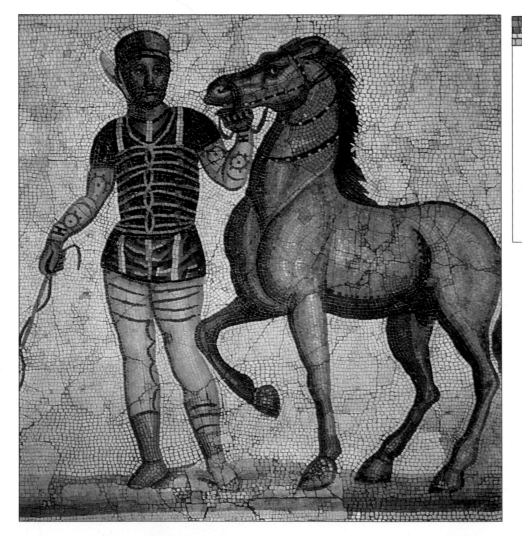

Mistakes in mosaics

Some of the Roman mosaics that survive today have mistakes in their patterns. They were probably made by learners, or **apprentices**.

Painting and writing

Painters often decorated the walls of Roman houses with pictures. Their assistants ground up all kinds of minerals to make coloured paints. The artists usually put the paint straight on to the plastered walls. Sometimes they painted the picture on wooden panels, which were easier to remove.

Writers, too, worked with a variety of materials. Sometimes they wrote on hand-made paper scrolls, which were made from an Egyptian river reed called **papyrus**. A thicker paper, or parchment,

▼ This wall painting is from Pompeii. It shows scenes from a garden. Sometimes artists painted flat walls of houses with false windows and columns, to trick the eye.

▲ This wall painting from a Roman villa shows an everyday scene in a very lifelike manner.

was called **vellum**. It was made from animal skins. People also sent messages by scratching letters on small, wax-covered boards, or **tablets**. Stonecarvers designed the most beautiful writing. They made the elegant capital letters that we still see on public monuments.

◄ These Roman inkwells are made of bronze. Ink was made from soot or from the black liquid squirted out by cuttlefish.

CLOTHES AND FASHION

Weaving and textiles

The Romans used woven material, or **textiles**, for clothing, for hangings to decorate the home, for outside blinds which provided shade and for tough sailcloth.

A plant called **flax** was used for making linen cloth. It was grown in Egypt. Cotton and silk were rare and costly imports from Asia. The most important material was wool, which was produced all over the empire. Roman landowners went to some trouble to improve the quality of the wool from their sheep.

After the sheep were sheared, the wool had to be washed to remove its natural greasiness and any dirt. It was then dried and wound on to a stick called a distaff, which spinners held under their arm. The woollen threads, or fibres, were pulled out and tied to a weighted stick called a drop spindle. As this spun round and round, it twisted the wool into a long thread, or yarn.

Weaving was done on a large, upright wooden frame called a loom. The weavers wound the **warp** threads around the top

▼ This picture, drawn from a Roman carving, shows a woman using a drop spindle.

Cloth of many colours

● Dyes were made from leaves, roots, berries, minerals and even shellfish, such as whelks.
● Saffron from crocuses made a yellow dye.
● Leaves from a plant called woad made a blue dye.
● The roots of a plant called madder made a red dye.
● A shellfish called murex provided a special purple dye. It was made at Tyre in the eastern Mediterranean. Only high-ranking Romans were allowed to wear Tyrian purple.

crossbar of the loom. Then they hung weights on them, or fixed them to a bottom crossbar. They passed the **weft** threads from side to side between the warp threads.

The woven cloth was often loose and baggy. It was taken to a workshop where it was washed with water and soda. The people trampled it underfoot until the fibres tightened up. This process is called fulling.

The cloth was then stretched, dried and bleached

▼ A modern copy of a Roman loom

▲ This relief shows customers checking the quality of textiles. It was carved during the early days of the Roman empire. Later, the Romans brought much of their cloth from Gaul, Britain, Greece and North Africa.

to whiten it. It might be fluffed up with prickly **teasels**, or beaten with wooden mallets to make it thicker. Then it was trimmed with shears and pressed.

● In Roman times, women spun wool and still wove some of it into cloth at home. However, the textile business was growing across the empire. More and more weaving, and nearly all the fulling and dyeing, was done in town workshops.
● Woollen fleeces, yarn or finished textiles were soaked with mineral salts called mordants. The salts helped to fix the dyes. Dyeing workshops had wood-fired boilers or vats made of stone lined with copper.

▲ This stone carving is about 2000 years old. It comes from an altar, and it shows the family of an emperor. The carving gives us an idea of how rich men, women and children dressed at that time.

Clothing

The most common item of clothing in ancient Rome was a simple **tunic**. It was worn by children, by most working people and by slaves.

Boys of the more important families could wear a white woollen robe called a ***toga***. It had a purple stripe around the edge. At the age of 16 a young man gave his boy's clothes to the gods at a special ceremony. It was a sign of growing up.

All men who were free citizens of Rome had the right – and duty – to wear a plain *toga* over their tunic. Important men wore a tunic with a thin purple stripe. Senators wore a *toga* with a thick purple stripe. The *toga* was a six-metre length of heavy cloth. It was hard to put on and not easy to wear. The *toga* went out of fashion in the later years of the empire.

Roman men never wore trousers. They thought these garments were fit only for Persian women or Celtic warriors! However, working men did tie strips of cloth around their legs, and Roman soldiers wore knee-length leather breeches.

For underwear, women and men wore loincloths and under-tunics or shifts. Women might also wear a type of brassière.

The full-length woman's over-dress was called a *stola*. It was high-waisted and fastened at the shoulder. Sometimes a woman wore a shawl called a *palla* over her head and shoulders.

◀ This beautiful ivory carving dates from the later days of the Roman empire. Roman girls wore white until they were married. Brides wore white dresses and red veils. Married women often wore colourful dresses with embroidered hems. Fashions changed much more slowly then than they do today.

Holding the fort

● Vindolanda was a Roman fort on Hadrian's Wall, in northern Britain. Archaeologists have found account books and letters from the fort.

● These include orders for warm tunics, capes and cloaks. There are requests for blankets, rugs and supplies of wool.

● There is even a letter to a soldier from home, saying that the writer has sent him pairs of woolly socks and underpants. Socks and stockings were worn only in the cold north.

▲ This Roman huntsman wears a practical short tunic, which has been dyed and decorated with patterns.

▼ Female athletes wore leather briefs and brassières, very like the bikini of today.

Boots and shoes

Walking through any Roman town, you would have seen shoemakers, cobblers and skilled leatherworkers. They cut and hammered out the leather in their workshops.

The leather itself was usually prepared out of town in a **tannery**. There the raw skins, or hides, of cattle and horses were soaked in tubs or vats of **tannin** to turn them into tough leather. The smell of the tanneries was disgusting.

Most Romans wore leather sandals. There were many designs of straps and soles, some with hobnails. Some slippers had criss-cross laces. In country areas, both men and women needed sturdy boots, clogs or shoes.

▲ A Roman shoemaker cuts out a sole from tough leather.

▼ This style of leather shoe was in fashion in Roman Britain, about 1800 years ago.

'Little Boots'

● From AD 37 until AD 41, the emperor of Rome was Gaius Caesar Augustus Germanicus. He was better known by his childhood nickname, Caligula ('little boots').

● This name came from the army boots, or *caligae*, which he wore as a child. He was brought up in an army camp. Caligula grew up to be a mad and murderous ruler.

◀ This young woman writer is wearing a jewelled hairnet, held in place with a gold headband. The wall painting comes from Pompeii.

Hats and sunshades

The Romans did not often wear hats. They preferred to shelter from rain or sun under hoods or shawls. However, in many remote parts of the empire local fashions remained popular. Men and women wore caps, bonnets, fur hats or broad-brimmed hats. Some of the finest craft work went into Roman women's headdresses. These included circlets of silver or gold, and jewelled headbands and hairnets.

In hot sun, a Roman might stay cool under a sunshade, although it would not fold up like today's umbrellas. Some people might have used a peacock feather fan to cool themselves.

▶ Hoods kept out the cold in northern parts of the Roman empire. Hooded cloaks were made in Gaul and Britain. They were worn over the tunic. This man also wears strips of cloth around his legs.

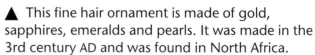

Jewellery

Green emeralds, blood-red garnets, creamy pearls, glassy black jet, dark yellow amber from the Baltic – the Romans loved jewellery. All over the empire there were workshops where craftworkers melted down gold and polished precious stones. Some of the finest work came from eastern cities such as Alexandria and Antioch.

Both men and women wore brooches to fasten their cloaks. They often had several rings on their fingers. These might have included wedding rings and **signet rings**. Women wore earrings, bracelets and anklets, as well as necklaces or pendants.

Make-up and hair styles

Some rich Roman women spent long hours each day putting on make-up, or cosmetics, and having their hair styled. Household slaves brought them ointments and lotions in little jars. There was red lipstick and **rouge** for the cheeks, made of a red earth powder called red ochre. Eyeshadow was made with ashes.

No rich woman wanted to look like some out-of-doors country girl. She wanted her face to look pale, so she powdered it with chalk or lead. Lead was actually a dangerous poison. In the later years of the empire, the fashion was for elaborate, piled-up hair styles.

▲ This fine hair ornament is made of gold, sapphires, emeralds and pearls. It was made in the 3rd century AD and was found in North Africa.

▶ This Roman signet ring was found in Britain. It is made out of iron. The red stone, called jasper, is carved with the initials 'VS'. It is decorated with the head of the Greek hero, Hercules.

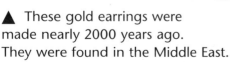

▲ These gold earrings were made nearly 2000 years ago. They were found in the Middle East.

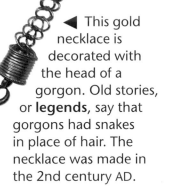

◄ This gold necklace is decorated with the head of a gorgon. Old stories, or **legends**, say that gorgons had snakes in place of hair. The necklace was made in the 2nd century AD.

Most Roman men wore their hair short. They had it cut at barbers' shops, which were great centres of news and gossip. Beards soon went out of fashion. Many men made a daily visit to the public baths, where slaves scraped and oiled their bodies.

▲ Slaves are waiting on their wealthy Roman mistress as she dresses for the day. They are bringing her a mirror of silver or bronze. This marble relief comes from the Moselle region of Germany.

◄ This woman lived in Egypt during the 2nd century AD. She is wearing earrings made of emeralds and gold with a matching necklace. The second necklace carries a small jewelled pendant. Her hair is tied back.

Curls and wigs

● Roman women liked to wear hairpieces and wigs. Wig-makers imported large amounts of cut black hair from India.

Men and women sometimes dyed their hair. In the later days of the empire some men also had their hair curled with hot irons.

FESTIVALS AND HOLIDAYS

The ancient Romans loved public holidays. There were religious festivals and family festivals. Sometimes there were grand parades to celebrate a legion's victory in a distant part of the empire. At one period, there were no fewer than 159 official public holidays in the year!

The craftworkers left their workshops and went to watch a chariot race, or fights between **gladiators**. Some workers might go to an open-air theatre to see a play.

However, workers who had good business sense would be out selling their wares to the crowds on the street. Everyone liked to look their best for a holiday. They would put on their finest clothes and show off their jewellery.

Here are some suggestions for items you could make for different Roman festivals and special events.

Wear a dolphin brooch

Roman men and women fastened their cloaks with beautiful brooches. These were often in the shape of animals. Make this dolphin brooch for 23 July, the festival of the sea god Neptune.

You will need: ● a pencil ● some stiff card ● scissors ● a gold marker (or gold paint or spray) ● sticky tape and a safety pin.

1. Copy the dolphin shape, below left, on to a piece of stiff card.

2. Cut out the shape with scissors.

3. Colour it gold, with a marker, or with paint or spray. Leave it to dry if necessary.

4. Tape a safety pin on to the back of the card.

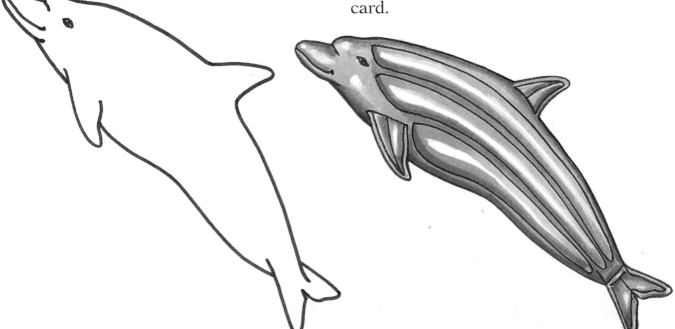

Design a mosaic

The goddess of the corn and the harvest was called Ceres. We still use her name in the word 'cereal'. There were several festivals to honour Ceres each year. Public games were held during the Cerialia, between 12 and 19 April. In August, women would dress in white and not eat for nine days. Then they offered the first fruits of the harvest to the goddess. Make a design in the style of a mosaic, showing Ceres and all the goodness of a Roman harvest.

You will need: ● scissors ● a pencil ● paper of many different colours (you could use pages from a magazine) ● glue ● a large sheet of stiff card.

1. Use a pencil to draw an outline of your design on to the card. You might draw the head of Ceres in the middle. You could show her as a young woman, and draw a ring of barley around her.

2. Around the rest of the area you could sketch in sheaves of wheat, grapes, leeks, celery, apples, figs and olive branches.

3. Cut up the paper into enough tiny pieces to cover the sheet of card, keeping the various colours in separate piles.

4. Stick the pieces of paper on to the card to make up the picture.

Crowning glory

Victory parades for the army were called 'triumphs'. The legions marched through Rome, followed by captured prisoners and treasure. There were special rewards for the bravest soldiers.

A soldier who had saved someone's life won a wreath of oak-leaves. The first soldier to go over a city wall during a **siege** won a golden crown. The crown was shaped like a wall. Why not give yourself a bravery award?

You will need: ● a large sheet of card ● a pencil ● scissors ● sticky tape ● a stapler ● paints ● 1 metre of red ribbon about 2cm wide.

1. Cut out two strips of card, about 10 cm wide and long enough to wrap around your head.

2. Copy the designs below on to the strips, and cut them out.

cork-oak-leaf crown

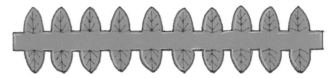

over-the-wall crown

3. Paint the wreath boldly in green, outlined with brown. Let it dry. Join the two ends together with sticky tape. Staple a red ribbon to the joint as shown.

4. Paint the crown gold, outlined with black. Let it dry. Staple a length of red ribbon around the bottom edge. Join the two ends of the crown together with sticky tape.

Make an actor's mask

On public holidays, thousands of people crowded into the theatres to watch their favourite actors appear in plays. The audience sat on rows, or tiers, of semi-circular stone benches. The actors wore masks. If the play was a sad one, a tragedy, the masks were sad too. Smiling masks showed that the play was a comedy. Make your own comic and tragic mask to use in a performance.

You will need: ● 2 large sheets of card (at least 21cm by 29cm) ● a pencil ● scissors ● string or tape ● poster paints.

1. Use a pencil to copy the mask designs on to the sheets of card. Draw them the size of your face.

2. Cut out the mask shapes and paint them. Leave them to dry.

3. Make holes in the sides of the masks.

4. Thread knotted string or tape through the holes so that you can tie each mask on.

Saturnalia!

This festival, in honour of the god Saturn, took place towards the end of December. It became more and more popular, until the holiday lasted for seven days.

Children had a holiday from school. No one had to wear those uncomfortable *togas* during this holiday. All the laws on gambling were ignored, and no criminals were punished. People held parties and feasts, and masters waited upon their servants.

Everybody exchanged gifts, from silver dishes to jewellery. Traditionally, the gifts also included wax candles and small clay figures. Make a clay figure as a present.

You will need: ● modelling clay

1. Look at the models in the picture. Use your clay to make a model of the one you like best, or of someone you know.

GLOSSARY

adze: A metal tool used to shape wood or stone.

alloy: A mixture of two or more metals.

anvil: A metal block on which hot metal is hammered into a shape.

apprentice: Someone who is learning a trade.

archaeologist: Someone who studies the past by digging up or examining ancient ruins or remains.

armourer: Someone who makes weapons and armour.

blacksmith: A worker of iron.

chisel: A sharp metal tool used for chipping at wood or stone.

craft: Any trade or pastime in which people use skill to make things by hand.

cutlery: Knives and spoons (the Romans did not use forks).

deposits: Parts of the earth where minerals have collected naturally.

drill: A metal tool which bores holes.

earthenware: Plain, unglazed pottery.

empire: A group of countries which are ruled by a single emperor or government.

excavation: Carefully digging up ancient ruins and remains.

flax: A plant whose tough, stringy fibres are used to make linen.

frieze: A long patterned band or picture used to decorate a wall.

furnace: A very hot oven used for melting ores.

gild: To cover with a very thin layer of gold, gold dust or gold-coloured paint.

gladiator: A fighter, often a slave, who fought in public entertainments.

guild: An organization of people working in the same trade. Members of the Roman guilds, or *collegia*, also had religious and public duties.

kiln: An oven where you can bake material such as clay to a very high temperature.

legend: An old story which many people believe, even though it might not be quite true.

legion: Part of the Roman army. There were about 4200 soldiers in a legion. The soldiers were divided into many smaller groups.

lime: A chalky substance used in making glass.

minerals: Useful substances which can extracted from the earth, such as metals, gemstones and fuels.

mould: A hollow form which gives its shape to materials such as clay, plaster, molten metals or glass.

ore: Rock which contains valuable metals.

papyrus: A reed which grows in the River Nile, in Africa. Strips of it were pressed or hammered together to make a type of paper.

plane: A wooden tool with a metal blade it in, used for shaving and smoothing wood.

relief: A picture or decoration raised from its flat background, such as a stone carving on a wall.

rouge: Powder to redden the cheeks, 'blusher'.

siege: When an army surrounds a town so that no one can go in or out, and no supplies of food or weapons can reach the people. The aim was to starve the people into surrender.

signet ring: A ring with a personal design which can be pressed into sealing wax.

smelt: To separate metal from ore at high temperatures.

soda: Sodium carbonate, a substance used in glassmaking.

tablets: Wooden boards coated with wax, about the size of a modern book. Writing was scratched into the wax.

tannery: A place where leather is made from raw animal hides.

tannin: A chemical found in various tree barks and plants. It is used in leathermaking.

teasel: The prickly head of a plant used to raise the surface, or nap, of cloth.

terracotta: Unglazed clay that has been baked until it is hard.

textile: Any material that is made up of woven threads.

***toga*:** A section of cloth with a curved edge. It was folded and draped as a robe.

trademark: A mark or symbol showing where or by whom a product was made.

tunic: A simple garment like a long shirt.

vellum: A writing surface made from calf or lambskin. It was rubbed with chalk to make it smooth.

warp: The upright or lengthwise threads on a loom.

weft: The yarn threaded from side to side on a loom.

Further reading

Costume and Clothes, Penelope Paul, 'Legacies' series (Wayland Publishers Limited, 1995)
In Ancient Rome, Philip Steele, 'Food and Feasts' series, (Wayland Publishers Limited, 1994)
Roman Times, M. Corbishley, 'Clues to the Past' series, (Watts Publishing Group, 1993)
Romans, N. Baxter, 'Craft Topics' series, (Watts Publishing Group, 1992)
The Romans and Pompeii, Philip Steele, 'Hidden Worlds' series, (Zoë Books Limited, 1994)

INDEX